The

Michelle Obama

Unofficial White House Guide to Rights and Privilege of

Transgender

Persons

Compiled by Richard Saunders with publicly accessible documents from the President Obama Administration.

The Michelle Obama Transgender Guide - 2

Table of Contents

Transgender Female Health Warnings........................3

HIV Among Transgender People..............................11

I Think I Might Be - Now What Do I Do?.....................17

Transgender Military Service Member Policy..............27

OSHA Guide to Restroom Access for Transgender Workers
....30

Recognizing the Unique Challenges of Transgender
   Women of Color...37

Our Commitment to Improving Outcomes in the
   Transgender Community...................................40

Marking Transgender Day of Remembrance...............43

Index...46

The Michelle Obama Transgender Guide - 3

Transgender Female Health Warnings

Facts from the Veterans Administration

Transgender Veterans who identify as women face increased health risks and unique challenges in accessing quality healthcare. VHA strives to be a national leader in the provision of LGBT health care and assure that high-quality care is provided in a sensitive, respectful environment. Research shows that transgender identity is about 5 times more common among Veterans than non-Veterans. Many transgender Veterans receive care at VHA. The following is a list of the top things transgender female Veterans should discuss with their VHA healthcare provider.

1. COME OUT TO YOUR HEALTH CARE PROVIDER

In order to provide you with the best care possible, your VHA doctor should know you are transgender. It should prompt him/her to ask specific questions about you and offer appropriate health screens. If your provider does not seem comfortable with you as a transgender woman, ask for another VHA provider. It's important for you to be able to trust your healthcare provider. Tell your provider about the medicines you have taken and the surgeries you may have had. If your providers know what has happened with you in the past, they will be better able to give you the best treatment today. Coming out to your providers is an important step to being healthy. For frequently asked questions about privacy, see Your Privacy Matters on page 3.

2. HORMONE TREATMENT

Talk with your VHA provider about hormone treatment. If you are starting hormones for the first time, ask about the things you need to watch out for while taking these medicines, such as blood clots, swelling, high blood sugar and blood pressure. Be sure to take the hormones only as prescribed by your provider.

3. MENTAL HEALTH

Depression, anxiety, PTSD, and other mental health problems affect transgender Veterans at higher rates than non-transgender Veterans. Transgender women may also experience chronic stress from discrimination. Living with this stress can cause depression and anxiety and may also contribute to thoughts of suicide. Many transgender Veterans have suicidal thoughts and even attempt suicide. These problems may be more severe for transgender women who remain "in the closet" or who do not have adequate social supports. Culturally-appropriate mental health services for transgender women for the prevention, early detection, and treatment of these conditions should be available at your VHA. If you are in crisis, please call 911, go to your nearest Emergency Room, or call the Veterans Crisis Line at 1-800-273- 8255 (press "1" after you call).

4. SUBSTANCE USE/ALCOHOL

Heavy drinking and substance use are common among transgender Veterans. Alcohol and drug misuse can lead to serious health, relationship, employment, and legal problems. Problems with drinking or drug use may occur in response to stress, and/or in combination with PTSD, depression, or other medical conditions. Fortunately, there are proven methods to help Veterans recover from alcohol or drug misuse, including mutual help groups and more intensive treatments. VHA has many resources to help Veterans (including transgender Veterans) and their loved ones, answer questions, find support, get treatment, and recover.

5. TOBACCO USE

Transgender Veterans use tobacco at much higher rates than non-transgender Veterans. Tobacco-related health problems include lung disease and lung cancer, heart disease, high blood pressure, and many other serious problems, especially in transgender women taking hormones. All transgender women should be screened for and offered culturally-appropriate prevention and cessation programs for tobacco use. VHA has programs to help you quit smoking. Talk to your provider about how VHA can help or call 1-855-QUIT-VET to get started. Get text messages to help you quit smoking from SmokefreeVET—text the word VET to 47848 or visit http:// smokefree.gov/VET to sign up.

6. SEXUALLY TRANSMITTED INFECTIONS (STIS)

STIs occur in sexually active transgender Veterans at a high rate. Some STIs can be cured (syphilis, gonorrhea, chlamydia, pubic lice), and some can be effectively treated but not cured (HIV, hepatitis, human papilloma virus, herpes). Condom use reduces the risk of STIs. Risk of exposure increases with the number of sexual partners. Because you can have an STI without symptoms, and transmit it to others, screening is important.

» HIV/AIDS

Transgender women who have sex with men are at an increased risk of HIV infection. Condom use can reduce the risk of receiving or transmitting HIV. Pre-Exposure Prophylaxis (PrEP) is one strategy for reducing the risk of getting infected with HIV. If you are not HIV positive, discuss with your VHA provider whether PrEP is best. If you are HIV positive, you need to be in care with an HIV provider.

» HEPATITIS IMMUNIZATION AND SCREENING

Transgender women who have sex with men are at increased risk of exposure to the viruses that cause the serious liver conditions known as hepatitis. These infections can lead to very serious long-term issues such as liver failure and liver cancer. Immunizations are available to prevent two of the three most serious viruses (hepatitis A and B). Condom use and not sharing needles are effective at reducing the risk of viral hepatitis and are currently the only means of prevention for the hepatitis C virus. If you have hepatitis C, talk to your provider about the new treatments that can cure this infection.

» HUMAN PAPILLOMA VIRUS (HPV)

Of all the sexually transmitted infections transgender women are at risk for, HPV—which causes anal and genital warts—is often thought to be little more than an unsightly inconvenience. However, these infections may play a role in the increased rates of anal cancers. Health professionals recommend routine screening including internal exams and/or anal pap smears. Talk to your VHA provider about whether screening is recommended.

7. CANCER

Transgender women may be at risk for some cancers. Screening for these cancers occurs across the life cycle and screening may occur less often if you are not "out" with your provider. It is very rare to develop cancer due to hormone treatment, but your provider will evaluate you for this possibility during your check-ups. Your provider will also check for possible cancer of your prostate (even after surgery), and breast tissue. Routine cancer screenings is part of quality VHA care.

8. FITNESS (DIET AND EXERCISE)

Problems with body image are common among transgender Veterans, including eating disorders such as bulimia or anorexia. Obesity also affects many transgender Veterans and can lead to a number of health problems, including diabetes, high blood pressure, joint problems, and heart disease. Regular exercise is part of a healthy lifestyle for transgender women. If you are planning to have surgery, your surgeon will want to be sure you are in good physical condition to do well during and after surgery. Talk to your VHA provider about the MOVE! Weight Management Program.

9. HEART HEALTH

Transgender Veterans are more likely than non-transgender Veterans to have high blood pressure and an increased risk of heart disease. Transgender Veterans are more likely than non-transgender Veterans to have experienced a heart attack or congestive heart failure. High blood pressure is a major risk factor for cardiovascular disease and can be affected by stress, including stress from discrimination. High blood pressure can be managed with healthy lifestyle changes and medications. Getting your blood pressure checked regularly is important because high blood pressure often has no symptoms.

10. INTIMATE PARTNER VIOLENCE (IPV)

IPV refers to violence and aggression between intimate partners which can include physical, sexual or psychological abuse or stalking. IPV can be a single event or last for many years. The impact of IPV can reach far beyond the actual or threatened violence or aggression. Military sexual trauma (MST) is the term used by the VA to refer to experiences of sexual assault or repeated, threatening sexual harassment that a Veteran experienced during her military service. Transgender Veterans are more likely than non-transgender

Veterans to have experienced MST. VHA has a number of resources available for transgender women who have experienced IPV, including effective therapies for mental health problems that commonly occur with IPV. Every VHA facility has providers knowledgeable about treatment for the after effects of MST.

11. OLDER TRANSGENDER WOMEN

Older transgender women have experienced stigma, discrimination and violence at higher rates than non-transgender women. Older transgender women who need assistance may experience discrimination in nursing homes or community living centers or live in fear of that discrimination. The VHA has non-discrimination policies in place to protect older transgender women and their families in VA facilities.

12. KIDNEY DISEASE

Transgender Veterans are more likely than non-transgender Veterans to have kidney disease. The kidneys filter wastes out of your blood to make urine. With kidney disease the kidneys filter blood poorly and wastes build up in the body. Diabetes and high blood pressure are the leading causes of kidney disease. Use of feminizing medications may worsen kidney disease.

YOUR PRIVACY MATTERS

I DON'T WANT ANYONE BESIDES MY PROVIDER TO KNOW THAT I'M TRANSGENDER. WILL THIS INFORMATION BE SHARED?

Your VHA provider has been trained to keep your conversations confidential. You can also ask that this information not be entered into your medical record, although medically necessary information must be included in your medical record (such as a medical diagnosis).

The Michelle Obama Transgender Guide - 9

Finding a provider you are comfortable with is essential to your health and wellness.

WHAT IF MY PROVIDER USES THE WRONG TERMS OR PRONOUNS WHEN REFERRING TO ME OR MY SPOUSE/PARTNER?

Your VHA provider may not know what terms you prefer to use. Let providers know how you describe yourself and your partner(s), and they will start to use those words. If they make a mistake, let them know! Your provider wants to make you feel comfortable, and using words that you prefer is an important first step.

DOES THE VHA HAVE RESOURCES TO HELP ME FIND A PROVIDER WHO IS COMFORTABLE WITH MY GENDER IDENTITY?

Yes! Each facility will soon have a LGBT Veteran Care Coordinator, who can help you find a culturally competent provider. In addition, many VA facilities have LGBT Veteran Web pages. For a list of those Web pages, see here: www.patientcare.va.gov/LGBT/VAFacilities.asp

To find the VHA medical center or Vet Center nearest you, call 1-877-222-8387 or visit www.va.gov/directory. Every VHA has a LGBT Veteran Care Coordinator to assure you have access to appropriate treatment. They can assist you with finding providers, answering questions, and reporting problems if you encounter them.

LGBT PROGRAM OFFICE The LGBT Program within the Office of Patient Care Services assists LGBT Veterans in accessing quality health care. Visit our website at http://go.usa.gov/cuth4

ADDITIONAL RESOURCES

ARE YOU A MEDICAL PROVIDER LOOKING FOR RESOURCES TO HELP PROVIDE CARE TO LGBT VETERANS?

Health Professionals Advancing LGBT Equality
www.glma.org

The Fenway Institute–The National LGBT Health Education Center www.lgbthealtheducation.org

ARE YOU A VETERAN LOOKING TO UNDERSTAND WHY YOUR SEXUAL ORIENTATION AND GENDER IDENTITY ARE IMPORTANT TO YOUR OVERALL CARE?

Centers for Disease Control and Prevention – LGBT Health www.cdc.gov/lgbthealth

DO YOU WANT MORE INFORMATION ON THE VA'S PATIENT CARE SERVICES LGBT PROGRAM?

The Lesbian, Gay, Bisexual and Transgender Program http://go.usa.gov/cuth4

ARE YOU A VETERAN LOOKING FOR GENERAL INFORMATION ABOUT THE PROGRAMS MENTIONED ABOVE?

Tobacco and Health www.publichealth.va.gov/smoking/index.asp

Viral Hepatitis www.hepatitis.va.gov

HIV/AIDS www.hiv.va.gov

MOVE! Weight Management Program www.move.va.gov

If you are in crisis, please call 911, go to your nearest Emergency Room, or call the Veterans Crisis Line at 1-800-273-8255 (press "1" after you call).

VISIT US WWW.PATIENTCARE.VA.GOV

HIV Among Transgender People

April 2016

Fast Facts

• Studies reveal high HIV prevalence rates among transgender women in the United States.

• Black/African American transgender women are more likely to have HIV than transgender women of other races/ethnicities.

• Many social and structural factors pose challenges to preventing HIV among transgender people.

Terminology

Transgender is an umbrella term for persons whose gender identity or expression (masculine, feminine, other) is different from their sex (male, female) at birth. Gender identity refers to one's internal understanding of one's own gender, or the gender with which a person identifies. Gender expression is a term used to describe people's outward presentation of their gender.

The Numbers

Because data for transgender people are not uniformly collected, information is lacking on how many transgender people in the United States are infected with HIV. However, data collected by local health departments and scientists studying these communities show high levels of HIV and racial/ethnic disparities.

• In 2013, a meta-analysis (Baral et al.) reported that the estimated HIV prevalence among transgender women was 22% in five high- income countries, including the United States.

- Findings from a systematic review (Herbst et al.) of 29 published studies showed that 28% of transgender women had HIV infection (4 studies), while 12% of transgender women self-reported having HIV (18 studies). This discrepancy suggests many transgender women living with HIV don't know their HIV status.

- In the systematic review, black/African American transgender women were most likely to test HIV positive, compared to those of other races/ethnicities: 56% of black/African American transgender women had positive HIV test results compared to 17% of white or 16% of Hispanic/Latina transgender women.

- Among the 3.3 million HIV testing eventsa reported to CDC in 2013, the highest percentages of newly identified HIV-positive persons were among transgender persons.

- Although HIV prevalence among transgender men is relatively low (0-3%), a 2011 study (Rowniak et al.) suggests that transgender men who have sex with men are at substantial risk for acquiring HIV. Prevention Challenges Individual behaviors alone do not account for the disparate HIV diagnoses among transgender people. Many cultural, socioeconomic, and health-related factors contribute to these diagnoses and prevention challenges in transgender communities.

Sexual behaviors and factors that may contribute to the high risk of HIV infection among transgender people include receptive anal sex without a condom or medicines to prevent HIV, a high prevalence of HIV in sexual networks, sex with multiple partners, and exchanging sex for drugs or money.

Other factors that contribute to high rates of HIV among transgender people include drug and alcohol abuse, mental health disorders, incarceration, homelessness, unemployment, lack of familial support, violence, stigma, discrimination, limited health care access, and negative health care encounters.

Many transgender people face social rejection and marginalization that excludes them from participating and functioning in society. Lack of legal recognition of gender identity can result in the denial of educational, employment, and housing opportunities. Some transgender people who experience poverty rely on sex work to meet their basic survival needs.

Insensitivity to transgender identity can be a barrier for those who are diagnosed with HIV and seek quality treatment and care services. Research shows transgender women with diagnosed HIV infection are less likely to be on antiretroviral therapy (ART) or achieve viral suppression. Furthermore, few health care providers receive adequate training or are knowledgeable about transgender health issues and their unique needs.

Transgender-specific data are limited. Currently, many federal, state, and local agencies inaccurately collect data about individuals' sex and gender. Using the two-step data collection method of asking for sex assigned at birth and current gender identity can help to increase the likelihood that transgender people will be accurately identified in HIV surveillance programs.

National Center for HIV/AIDS, Viral Hepatitis, STD, and TB Prevention Division of HIV/AIDS Prevention

Behavioral HIV prevention interventions developed for other at-risk groups with similar behaviors have been adapted for use with transgender people; however, their effectiveness is still unknown. There is a need for effective interventions that address the multiple co-occurring public health problems in transgender persons.

Transgender men's sexual health has been understudied. Additional research is needed to understand HIV risk behavior among transgender men, especially those who have sex with men.

The Michelle Obama Transgender Guide - 14

What CDC Is Doing

CDC and its partners are pursuing a high-impact prevention approach to achieve the goals of the National HIV/AIDS Strategy: Updated to 2020 (https://www.aids.gov/federal-resources/national-hiv-aids-strategy/nhas-update.pdf) and maximize the effectiveness of current HIV prevention methods among transgender people. Activities include:

- Funding community-based organizations (CBOs) to enhance their capacities to increase HIV testing, link transgender persons with diagnosed HIV infection to medical care, increase referrals to partner services, and provide prevention and support services for transgender persons at risk for or diagnosed with HIV.

- Supporting health department demonstration projects (http://www.cdc.gov/hiv/funding/announcements/ps15-1506/index.html) that provide pre-exposure prophylaxis (PrEP) (http://www.cdc.gov/hiv/risk/prep/index.html) support services and data-to-care activities prioritizing gay and bisexual men and transgender persons at substantial risk for acquiring HIV, particularly persons of color.

- Providing support and technical assistance to providers that help CBOs enhance structural interventions for transgender people (e.g., condom distribution, community mobilization, HIV testing, and coordinated referral networks and service integration).

- Developing Act Against AIDS (http://www.cdc.gov/actagainstaids/) communication materials to reach transgender people, including campaigns such as:

The Michelle Obama Transgender Guide - 15

- o **Doing It** (http://www.cdc.gov/actagainstaids/campaigns/doingit/index.html), which encourages all adults to get tested for HIV and know their status, and includes images (http://www.cdc.gov/actagainstaids/pdf/campaigns/doingit/getmaterials/posters/ doingit-chandimoore.pdf) and testimonial videos featuring transgender leaders.

- o **Let's Stop HIV Together** (http://www.cdc.gov/actagainstaids/campaigns/lsht/index.html), which raises awareness about HIV and fights stigma, and includes the stories (https://www.youtube.com/embed/9XXsTvYj22U) of transgender women.

- o **HIV Treatment Works** (http://www.cdc.gov/actagainstaids/campaigns/hivtreatmentworks/index.htm l), which encourages people living with HIV to stay in care, and features a transgender woman's story (https://www.youtube.com/embed/jo4KbnPrhEw) of staying healthy while living with HIV.

• Through its Capacity Building Assistance initiative, CDC is working with the Center of Excellence for Transgender Health to support National Transgender HIV Testing Day. This day recognizes the importance of routine HIV testing, status awareness, and continued focus on HIV prevention and treatment efforts among transgender people.

An HIV testing event is one or more HIV tests performed with a person to determine that person's HIV status. During one testing event, a person may be tested once or multiple times.

The Michelle Obama Transgender Guide - 16

Additional Resources

CDC-INFO 1-800-CDC-INFO (232-4636) www.cdc.gov/info

CDC HIV Website www.cdc.gov/hiv

CDC Act Against AIDS Campaign
www.cdc.gov/actagainstaids

I Think I Might Be – Now What Do I Do?

A Brochure by and for Transgender Youth

What Does It Mean to Be Transgender?

Transgender people feel that the gender to which they were born, or assigned at birth, does not fit them. Transgender people include people born female who iden- tify as male (female-to-male) and people born male who identify as female (male- to-female). Transgender people also include those who identify as "genderqueer," gender neutral, and/or gender-free—people who may not identify as either male or female. Transsexual people are those who choose to medically transition to the gender that is right for them. Cross-dressers are people who like to wear the clothes of another gender but who don't identify as another gender. You may find yourself identifying with one or more of these definitions pretty strongly or with none of them at all. No one has to rush to self-label, now or ever, and some people choose different labels that express more clearly how they see themselves.

How Do I Know if I'm Transgender?

I've always felt that I was a girl from the time I can first remember. Tasha, 19

I know I'm transgender because my brain knows it's female, and my body disagrees. Lana, 26

You may feel that you are more comfortable expressing yourself as a gender other than the gender you were born or assigned at birth. This gender might be the "oppo- site" of the gender you were born or assigned, or it might be neither male nor female but something else entirely! You may feel extremely uncomfortable with the gender-specific parts of your body. For example, you may have breasts and prefer not to have them. Or, you might not feel uncomfortable with your gender- specific body parts and, at the same time, feel a deep need to have other body parts.

You may feel more comfortable relating to people who perceive you as the gender you see yourself. You may simply feel you would be more truly yourself in another gender. People who are transgender may feel any or all of these emotions.

Am I Normal?

Since identifying myself as gender variant, I've met several other people my age who do, as well as lots of adults and also lots of other people who respect and love gender variant people. It may not be 'normal' to many people, but it's certainly healthy and widespread. And despite how it feels sometimes, I know I'm not the only one who feels the way I do. Mark, 18

It's normal for me. I couldn't stand living the rest of my life in my biological gender. I have been through reams of depression and low spots, and I have looked over my past; all these spots were caused by my deep need to be male. Riley, 22

Being transgender is as normal as being alive. Throughout history, many people have felt they were transgender. Transgender people are everywhere. They are teach- ers, doctors, construction workers, and waiters. They attend college, have chil- dren, and enjoy careers. You may interact with other transgender people every day and not know it! Certainly, being transgender is not "typical," and you may en- counter many people who do not understand or who feel uncomfortable or even discriminatory. However, you are certainly normal.

What's It Like to Be Young and Transgender?

Until I graduated from high school, it was horrible. Afterwards, it has been wonderful being seen as a woman wherever I go. Tasha, 20

Being young and transgender is just like being young and anything else. People our age accept us more readily than adults do, just like all other kids who are different. We do the same sorts of things that other kids do for fun, like playing sports, reading, writing, dating, and listening to music. Mark, 18

Most people will doubt your judgment because of your age. It may take a lot more talking to convince the 'adults' that you really know who you are. Chris, 19

Some young people who are transgender feel a great relief that they have discov- ered how they are most comfortable expressing themselves. Other youth feel frus- trated at being discriminated against or because they aren't yet able to transition. Still other young people find that being transgender is just one part of who they are and that they mostly think about all the things that many youth think about—school, dating, work, and family. There are as many ways to be young and transgender as there are ways to be young.

Whom Should I Tell?

I tell myself first, repeatedly. I keep it up until I bore myself. Once I'm bored, that means that my mind has completely come to terms with what I'm telling it. Then I'll be ready to tell others. Lana, 26

People had all sorts of reactions to my coming out. I lost a few friends and a lot of dates, but most people really tried to understand. Not everyone can get it, but with time and respect, people have learned to understand. Mark, 18

The first person I told was my girlfriend at the time; I told her before we got serious. I also told two close friends, my sister, and then my parents. After that, I considered myself out and didn't hide it anymore. Chris, 19

There is no obligation to tell anyone about your identity. However, many people find it very important to share who they are with others, especially if they plan to transition publicly. If you decide to share your identity, first tell people with whom you are comfortable and that you feel will understand. They might include a trusted teacher, counselor, sister, brother, parent, friend, or people at a youth group for gay, lesbian, bisexual, and transgender (GLBT) people. Some young people stop there and choose to transition more fully later in life, but other youth choose to begin to live full-time as their identified gender. If you choose to do this, you may need to come out to many different people. You should definitely look for support when going through this process, from a therapist, a youth group, friends, family, and others.

What Will Happen When I Come Out?

That depends on your family. Mine is fairly accepting of me and now, almost six years after I came out, mostly treats me as if I had been born a girl. Tasha, 19

The Michelle Obama Transgender Guide - 21

Coming out as trans was the hardest thing I've ever done. Sometimes, I can't believe I ever did it. Since then, everything has happened very quickly. It depends on your financial situation and what you want to do. I started therapy shortly after coming out, and within eight months (of coming out), I started testosterone therapy. What matters is that you do what you're ready to do and at the pace that makes you comfortable. Chris, 19

Some people feel relieved and happy when they come out. Others feel as if they are thrown into a lion's den, with challenges from parents, friends, and family. You will most likely experience a bit of both. Some transgender youth may face vio- lence at school or in their home. Please, make sure you have people you can talk to before you come out publicly, just for this reason. As you come out, you may find PFLAG (Parents, Families, and Friends of Lesbians and Gays) a useful resource. To make coming out easier, surround yourself with as much information, knowledge, and support as possible.

What Does It Mean to Transition? Should I Do It?

I know lots of people who have gone through medical transition and lots who haven't. I have not and I don't plan to. People whom I really care about tend to accept me as I am, so I don't feel that I need to. People who are happiest seem to just do what feels right for them. Mark, 18

I cannot continue living inside this male body. My femininity has been repressed too long. I need to be free of my cage. Lana, 26

I plan to medically transition. I don't feel that I will ever be comfortable being viewed as female. Riley, 22

Some people who come out as transgender are comfortable telling a close circle of friends. Other people choose to change their name, their pronouns, their style of dress, and their appearance to be congruent with their gender identity. Still others choose to take hormones and have surgery to medically alter their appearance. As you decide which, if any, steps to take, it can help to talk about these feelings with others, such as a mental health professional who is competent with gender identity issues, friends and family members you trust, and other transgender people. You should express yourself the way you feel most comfortable, without pressure from others.

Medical transition, the taking of hormones and having one or more surgeries, is a big step. For some, it is absolutely necessary. Most people who choose to transition medically strongly need identity and body to match. They want to be seen all the time and without question, as the gender they feel they are. To medically transition, you must first see a therapist and, in most cases, be diagnosed with Gender Identity Disorder. In most states, if you are under 18, you will need a parent's permission to undertake medical transition. If you plan to pursue medical transition, it is important that your transition be supervised by a medical professional. Undertaking transition without professional medical guidance can have severe health risks.

What Does Being Transgender Mean about My Sexual Orientation? Am I Gay or Straight or What?

I love guys!! I love to look at them; love how they move. I see myself as a heterosexual female. Tasha, 19

The Michelle Obama Transgender Guide - 23

I have always been attracted to females; but transgender people may be attracted to the opposite or to the same sex, and some are bisexual. Riley, 22

I thought I was a lesbian, because I was primarily attracted to women. Now I identify as 'queer' as an umbrella term, and avoid a label, though I am bisexual. Since coming out as male, my attraction has risen to other males. Mark, 19

Being transgender has to do with your gender identity: how you feel about who you are. It has nothing to do with your sexual orientation, which is about who attracts you. Some transgender people are attracted to men, some to women, some to other transgender people, and some to people regardless of their gender. People may define themselves with different labels, depending on who attracts them. For example, some transgender women who are attracted to men define themselves as straight, because they are attracted to the opposite gender. Other transgender women may feel attracted to men and define themselves as queer, to challenge the notion of "opposite" genders. Regardless of who attracts you, rest assured that many transgender people have happy, healthy relationships with people whom they love. Remember, you deserve to date people who respect you for who you are.

What about Sexually Transmitted Infections, HIV, and Pregnancy?

Remember that not having sex is the surest way to avoid unwanted pregnancy as well as HIV and other sexually transmitted infections (STIs). In fact, many youth choose to show affection through activities such as hugging, kissing, talking, and massage. If you choose to have sex, be responsible and talk with your partner about methods of protection for both of you. It's your responsibility and your partner's to protect both of you from unwanted outcomes.

The Michelle Obama Transgender Guide - 24

Transgender people can have a hard time finding safer sex information that speaks in language that reflects how they feel about their body. Because many may feel that their biological body doesn't reflect their gender identity, they may use differ- ent terms for body parts. Finding information that corresponds to an internal/emo- tional body concept can be difficult. No matter how transgender youth label sexual body parts, some or all of the following tips apply to each:

> ✔ For vaginal intercourse where there is a risk of pregnancy, use a latex or polyurethane condom and also another effective method of contraception, such as birth control pills or Depo-Provera.
>
> ✔ When touching someone else's genitals with your hands, use a latex or polyurethane barrier, such as surgical gloves.
>
> ✔ For oral sex, regardless of the genital area that the mouth touches, use a condom, a dental dam, or saran wrap.
>
> ✔ For anal intercourse, always use a latex or polyurethane condom with non-petroleum based lubrication, such as KY Jelly.
>
> ✔ When sharing sex toys, always use a latex or polyurethane condom with non-petroleum based lubrication.

Two important tips:

> ✔ Lubrication—Do not use petroleum- or oil-based lubricants with latex condoms because such lubricants weaken and/ or destroy the latex. Use only water-based lubricants, such as KY Jelly. Avoid using nonoxynol-9, because it may cause irritation and increase the risk of infection with HIV or other STIs.

Remember that blood-to-blood contact is the surest route for HIV infection. Sharing drug paraphernalia or needles—whether for piercing or tattooing the body, taking medications, or using drugs—is highly dangerous, since blood left on the used equipment or needle will come into contact with your blood as soon as you use the equipment or needle. Avoid sharing needles, razors, or other such paraphernalia, for any purpose.

How Do I Learn to Like Myself?

Coming to terms with who you really are is the most important step that anyone can make in this situation. How far you decide to go with it is important, but never as important as accepting yourself because accepting yourself will lead to liking yourself. Riley, 22

For me, it's a matter of continuing to focus on what I like about myself, what I think is great about my body, hanging out with positive people, and avoiding, as much as I can, the negative messages directed towards women (particularly transwomen) in the media. Brynn, 23

If you have just discovered or recognized that you are transgender, remember that you are normal and you are likeable, just as you are. With big discoveries come big life changes, and it is normal to feel nervous, apprehensive, and upset about the days ahead. Remember, too, that discovering something this important about your-self can be a truly amazing experience. You are one step ahead on the journey of discovering who you truly are, and with that journey, the world becomes full of possibilities as well as challenges. You are getting to know another part of your-self, and this is truly a wonderful opportunity!

The Michelle Obama Transgender Guide - 26

What Resources Exist for Transgender Youth?

Remember that you're not alone, and there is help out there:

www.youthresource.com is a Web site for youth who are gay, lesbian, bisexual, and transgender. It has some great information for transgender youth, as well as online message boards where you can talk with other young people who are facing the same or similar issues.

www.pflag.com offers lots of information for friends and family of transgender people.

www.youthresource.com/our_lives/youth_groups lists support groups. There, you may find a GLBTQ youth group in your area, offering friendship, support, and/or referral for professional care in your area.

Talking to others who face the same issues can help you learn to like yourself while, at the same time, giving you opportunities to help others.

ISBN: 0-913843-36-9 © 2004 Advocates for Youth, 2000 M Street, NW, Suite 750 Washington, DC 20036 USA Phone: 202.419.3420 Fax: 202.419.1448
www.advocatesforyouth.org www.youthresource.com

Transgender Military Service Member Policy

Implementation Fact Sheet

The Secretary's announcement on open service by transgender individuals involves two key documents. The first is a Directive Type Memorandum (DTM) that outlines Department policy with respect to military service by transgender individuals. The second document is a Department of Defense Instruction (DoDI) detailing the procedures by which a serving transgender Service member may transition gender. Both documents reflect the Department's finding that open service by transgender Service members, while being subject to the same standards and procedures as other members with regard to their medical fitness for duty, physical fitness, uniform and grooming, deployability, and retention, is consistent with military readiness.

Implementation Highlights

Today, the Department of Defense is ending the ban on transgender Americans serving in the United States military:

• This policy was crafted through a comprehensive and inclusive process that included the leadership of the Armed Services, medical and personnel experts across the Department, transgender Service members, outside medical experts, advocacy groups, and the RAND Corporation.

• Effective immediately, transgender Service members may serve openly, and they can no longer be discharged or otherwise separated from the military solely for being transgender individuals.

• These policies will be implemented in stages over the next 12 months—starting most immediately with addressing the needs of current Service members and their commanders, and followed by training for the entire force, and ultimately, beginning to admit transgender recruits.

Starting today:

• Otherwise qualified Service members can no longer be involuntarily separated, discharged, or denied reenlistment or continuation of service solely for being transgender individuals.

No later than 90 days from today (October 1, 2016):

• The Department will issue a training handbook for commanders, transgender Service members, and the force.

• The Department will issue medical guidance for providing transition related care to transgender Service members.

• The Military Health System will be required to provide transgender Service members with all medically necessary care related to gender transition, based on the guidance that is issued.

• Service members will be able to begin the process to officially change their gender in our personnel management systems.

Next, over the 9 months that follow (October 2016 – June 2017):

• Based on detailed guidance and training materials that will be issued, the Services will conduct training of the force—from commanders, to medical personnel, to the operating forces, and recruiters.

Not later than July 1, 2017:

• When the training of the force is complete, the military Services will begin accessing transgender applicants who meet all standards—holding them to the same physical and mental fitness standards as everyone else who wants to join the military.

• The gender identity of an otherwise qualified individual will not bar them from joining the military, from admission to our Service Academies, or from participating in ROTC or any other accession program.

• Our initial accession policy will require an individual to have completed any medical treatment that their doctor has determined is necessary in connection with their gender transition, and to have been stable in their preferred gender for 18 months, as certified by their doctor, before they can enter the military.

• This standard will be reviewed no later than 24 months from July 1, 2016 to ensure it reflects what more we learn as this is implemented, as well as the most updated medical information.

Policy Highlights

• Service members with a diagnosis from a military medical provider indicating that gender transition is medically necessary will be provided medical care and treatment for the diagnosed medical condition, in the same manner as other medical care and treatment.

• Gender transition in the military begins when a Service member receives a diagnosis from a military medical provider indicating that gender transition is medically necessary, and concludes when the Service member's gender marker is changed in the Defense Enrollment Eligibility Reporting System (DEERS) and the Service member serves and is recognized in the preferred gender.

• At that point, the Service member is responsible for meeting all applicable military standards in the preferred gender and will use berthing, bathroom, and shower facilities associated with their gender.

• Any discrimination against a Service member based on their gender identity is sex discrimination and may be addressed through the Department's equal opportunity channels.

OSHA Guide to Restroom Access for Transgender Workers

Core principle: All employees, including transgender employees, should have access to restrooms that correspond to their gender identity.

Introduction

The Department of Labor's (DOL) Occupational Safety and Health Administration (OSHA) requires that all employers under its jurisdiction provide employees with sanitary and available toilet facilities, so that employees will not suffer the adverse health effects that can result if toilets are not available when employees need them. This publication provides guidance to employers on best practices regarding restroom access for transgender workers. OSHA's goal is to assure that employers provide a safe and healthy working environment for all employees.

Understanding Gender Identity

In many workplaces, separate restroom and other facilities are provided for men and women. In some cases, questions can arise in the workplace about which facilities certain employees should use. According to the Williams Institute at the University of California-Los Angeles, an estimated 700,000 adults in the United States are transgender—meaning their internal gender identity is different from the sex they were assigned at birth (e.g., the sex listed on their birth certificate). For example, a transgender man may have been assigned female at birth and raised as a girl, but identify as a man. Many transgender people transition to live their everyday life as the gender they identify with. Thus, a transgender man may transition from living as a woman to living as a man. Similarly, a transgender woman may be assigned male at birth, but transition to living as a woman consistent with her gender identity. Transitioning is a different process for

everyone—it may involve social changes (such as going by a new first name), medical steps, and changing identification documents.

Why Restroom Access Is a Health and Safety Matter

Gender identity is an intrinsic part of each person's identity and everyday life. Accordingly, authorities on gender issues counsel that it is essential for employees to be able to work in a manner consistent with how they live the rest of their daily lives, based on their gender identity. Restricting employees to using only restrooms that are not consistent with their gender identity, or segregating them from other workers by requiring them to use gender-neutral or other specific restrooms, singles those employees out and may make them fear for their physical safety. Bathroom restrictions can result in employees avoiding using restrooms entirely while at work, which can lead to potentially serious physical injury or illness.

OSHA's Sanitation Standard

Under OSHA's Sanitation standard (1910.141), employers are required to provide their employees with toilet facilities. This standard is intended to protect employees from the health effects created when toilets are not available. Such adverse effects include urinary tract infections and bowel and bladder problems. OSHA has consistently interpreted this standard to require employers to allow employees prompt access to sanitary facilities. Further, employers may not impose unreasonable restrictions on employee use of toilet facilities.

Model Practices for Restroom Access for Transgender Employees

Many companies have implemented written policies to ensure that all employees—including transgender employees—have prompt access to appropriate sanitary facilities. The core belief underlying these policies is that all employees should be permitted to use the facilities that correspond with their gender identity. For example, a person who identifies as a man should be permitted to use men's restrooms, and a person who identifies as a woman should be permitted to use women's restrooms. The employee should determine the most appropriate and safest option for him- or herself.

The best policies also provide additional options, which employees may choose, but are not required, to use. These include:

- Single-occupancy gender-neutral (unisex) facilities; and

- Use of multiple-occupant, gender-neutral restroom facilities with lockable single occupant stalls.

Regardless of the physical layout of a worksite, all employers need to find solutions that are safe and convenient and respect transgender employees.

Under these best practices, employees are not asked to provide any medical or legal documentation of their gender identity in order to have access to gender-appropriate facilities. In addition, no employee should be required to use a segregated facility apart from other employees because of their gender identity or transgender status. Under OSHA standards, employees generally may not be limited to using facilities that are an unreasonable distance or travel time from the employee's worksite.

Other Federal, State and Local Laws

Employers should be aware of specific laws, rules, or regulations regarding restroom access in their states and/or municipalities, as well as the potential application of federal anti- discrimination laws.

The Equal Employment Opportunity Commission (EEOC), the Department of Justice (DOJ), DOL, and several other federal agencies, following several court rulings, have interpreted prohibitions on sex discrimination, including those contained in Title VII of the Civil Rights Act of 1964, to prohibit employment discrimination based on gender identity or transgender status. In April 2015, the DOL's Office of Federal Contract Compliance Programs (OFCCP) announced it would require federal contractors subject to Executive Order 11246, as amended, which prohibits discrimination based on both sex and gender identity, to allow transgender employees to use the restrooms and other facilities consistent with their gender identity. Also in April 2015, the EEOC ruled that a transgender employee cannot be denied access to the common restrooms used by other employees of the same gender identity, regardless of whether that employee has had any medical procedure or whether other employees' may have negative reactions to allowing the employee to do so. The EEOC held that such a denial of access constituted direct evidence of sex discrimination under Title VII.

However, a transgender employee will not be compelled to use only a specific restroom unless all other co-workers of the same gender identity are compelled to use only that same restroom.

The following is a sample of state and local legal provisions, all reaffirming the core principle that employees should be allowed to use the restrooms that correspond to their gender identity.

District of Columbia: Rule 4-802 of the D.C. Municipal Regulations prohibits discriminatory practices in regard to restroom access. Individuals have the right to use facilities consistent with their gender identity. In addition, single-stall restrooms must have gender-neutral signage. D.C. Municipal Regulations 4-802, "Restrooms and Other Gender Specific Facilities," available at: http://www.dcregs.dc.gov/Gateway/RuleHome.Aspx?uleNumber=4-802.

Iowa: The Iowa Civil Rights Commission requires that employers allow employees access to restrooms in accordance with their gender identity, rather than their assigned sex at birth.

For more information refer to: "Sexual Orientation & Gender Identity – An Employer's Guide to Iowa Law Compliance," Iowa Civil Rights Commission, available at: https://icrc.iowa.gov/sites/files/civil_rights/publications/2012/SOGIEmpl.pdf

Vermont: The Vermont Human Rights Commission requires that employers permit employees to access bathrooms in accordance with their gender identity.

For more information refer to: "Sex, Sexual Orientation, and Gender Identity: A Guide to Vermont's Anti-Discrimination Law for Employers and Employees," Vermont Human Rights Commission, available at: http://hrc.vermont.gov/sites/hrc/files/pdfs/other%20reports/trans%20employment%20brochure%20 7-13-12.pdf.

Washington: The Washington State Human Rights Commission requires employers that maintain gender-specific restrooms to permit transgender employees to use the restroom that is consistent with their gender identity. Where single occupancy restrooms are available, the Commission recommends that they be designated as "gender neutral."

The Michelle Obama Transgender Guide - 35

For more information refer to: "Guide to Sexual Orientation and Gender Identity and the Washington State Law Against Discrimination," available at: http://www.hum.wa.gov/ Documents/Guidance/GuideSO20140703.pdf .

Additional Information

• American Psychological Association. Answers to your questions about transgender people, gender identity and gender expression, 2011: http://www.apa.org/topics/lgbt/ transgender.aspx.

• Transgender Law Center's model employer policy, with an extensive section on restrooms, can be found at: http://transgenderlawcenter. org/wp-content/uploads/2013/12/model- workplace-employment-policy-Updated.pdf.

• "Restroom Access for Transgender Employees" on Human Rights Campaign website: http://www.hrc.org/resources/entry/ restroom-access-for-transgender-employees.

• National Gay and Lesbian Task Force and the National Center for Transgender Equality. National Transgender Discrimination Survey, 2011: http://endtransdiscrimination.org/ report.html.

How OSHA Can Help

OSHA has a great deal of information to assist employers in complying with their responsibilities under the law. Information on OSHA requirements and additional health and safety information, including information on OSHA's Sanitation standard, is available on the agency's website (www.osha.gov).

Workers have a right to a safe workplace (www.osha.gov/workers.html#2). The law requires employers to provide their employees with working conditions that are free of known dangers. An employer's duty to provide a safe workplace includes the duty to provide employees with toilet facilities that are sanitary and available, so that employees can use them when they need to do so.

Disclaimer: This document is not a standard or regulation, and it creates no new legal obligations. It contains recommendations as well as descriptions of mandatory safety and health standards. The recommendations are advisory in nature, informational in content, and are intended to assist employers in providing a safe and healthful workplace. The Occupational Safety and Health Act requires employers to comply with safety and health standards and regulations promulgated by OSHA or by a state with an OSHA-approved state plan. In addition, the Act's General Duty Clause, Section 5(a)(1), requires employers to provide their employees with a workplace free from recognized hazards likely to cause death or serious physical harm.

Recognizing the Unique Challenges of Transgender Women of Color

April 9, 2015 at 2:40 PM ET by Tina Tchen

Summary:

Assistant to the President Tina Tchen reflects on the historic steps this Administration has taken to afford greater protections for this community in just the past few months.

During Women's History Month, the White House Office of Public Engagement and the Council on Women and Girls have honored the achievements of women across the country and throughout history, while continuing the conversations about the challenges women across the nation still face. On March 31 -- National Transgender Day of Visibility -- I had the honor of speaking with leaders of the transgender women of color community during the White House's first-ever discussion solely focused on the challenges this community faces.

Community organizers, non-profit leaders, and policy advocates from all over the country shared their stories and spoke about the issues that uniquely affect transgender women of color. We heard from panelists on issues ranging from employment and economic opportunity, to family and intimate partner violence, to access to health care. These frank conversations helped to shine a light on the work left to be done, and possible community and government solutions.

Attendees also heard from Roy Austin Jr, Deputy Assistant to the President for the Office of Urban Affairs, Justice, and Opportunity, about the steps taken by the Administration to better protect the rights of transgender people, including LGBT-specific recommendations made in the report by the President's Task Force for 21st Century Policing that urge police departments to foster better relationships with and better statistical reporting of the transgender community.

The Michelle Obama Transgender Guide - 38

Roy also spoke about the Matthew Shepard and James Byrd, Jr. Hate Crimes Prevention Act, signed by President Obama in 2009, which expanded hate crimes law to include gender identity and sexual orientation and requires the FBI to publish statistics on hate crimes against transgender people.

I am proud to reflect on the historic steps this Administration has taken to afford greater protections for this community in just the past few months. Just yesterday, President Obama's Executive Order on LGBT Workplace Discrimination went into effect, prohibiting federal contractors and subcontractors from discriminating on the basis of sexual orientation and gender identity. On April 3, the Department of Justice filed an important brief as part of ongoing litigation in Georgia that advocated that prison officials have the obligation to assess and treat gender dysphoria just as they would any other medical or health condition. On March 31, the CDC announced $185 million for grant opportunities for HIV prevention among transgender people and gay and bisexual men, with a particular focus on the unique needs of people of color. The Department of Housing and Urban Development issued new guidance in February designed to better serve LGBT Americans seeking to obtain a home loan and to ensure appropriate placement of transgender individuals in homeless shelters. And in December, Attorney General Eric Holder announced the Department of Justice's position that the protections against sex discrimination under Title VII of the Civil Rights Act of 1964 extend to claims of discrimination based on gender identity, including transgender status.

Despite these significant steps, there is more work to be done. Though Women's History Month is over, I look forward to continuing conversations around the safety, health, and well-being of all women, including transgender women of color.

You should also read:

- We the People Petition Response: On Conversion Therapy
- Secretary Tom Perez: Another Step Toward Equality for LBGT Workers
- Valerie Jarrett: Protecting LBGT Workers Means Protecting All Workers
- Fellowship of the Minds - https://goo.gl/WEGPVd

Tina Tchen

Assistant to the President and Chief of Staff to the First Lady

Our Commitment to Improving Outcomes in the Transgender Community

April 1, 2016 at 10:22 AM ET by Dr. Amy Lansky and Raffi Freedman-Gurspan

Summary:

Find out what happened when The White House hosted a consultation with advocates on effectively addressing HIV in the transgender community.

This week, as National LGBT Health Awareness Week comes to a close, we wanted to recognize the ongoing work and challenges to improve the lives of transgender Americans. In February, we held the first-ever White House consultation on HIV among transgender people. The consultation brought community leaders, researchers, and advocates from across the country together with Federal agency partners to discuss issues transgender people face, and what the Federal government can do to reduce their risk of acquiring HIV, support them in accessing HIV care, and improve their lives.

Recognizing that transgender women are among the groups at highest risk for HIV infection in the U.S., when we released the updated National HIV/AIDS Strategy last summer, we committed to developing an indicator on HIV among transgender persons. As we undertake the process of developing this new indicator, we're doing a robust review of the literature, and considering the science, expert advice, and stakeholder input to identify the best way to measure and monitor HIV in transgender people. This is critical because if we can't measure something, we can't understand where to target our efforts and which are most effective. The consultation last month was part of our ongoing effort to inform the development of the transgender indicator and to involve key stakeholders and leaders in the development process.

At the consultation, we heard about what data we do and do not have on the transgender community at the Federal level. In the Ryan White HIV/AIDS Program, for example, Dr. Laura Cheever of HRSA highlighted that data on transgender clients is collected and analyzed each year. However, the data show that despite high overall rates of retention in care and viral suppression (80% and 81% of clients, respectively) in the program, transgender clients are experience slightly lower rates (78% and 74%, respectively).

In addition, Dr. Eugene McCray from CDC noted that overall, we have limited HIV surveillance data on how many transgender people in the United States are living with HIV because data for this population are not consistently collected. However, data collected by some local health departments and scientists studying these communities show high HIV prevalence and racial/ethnic disparities among transgender populations. Data suggest that around 28% of transgender women are living with HIV and that African American transgender women have higher rates than other groups of transgender women. This high HIV prevalence is one of the reasons we identified transgender women in the updated Strategy as a population on which we need to focus our efforts.

We know that this community experiences a spectrum of issues that exacerbate the risk for HIV acquisition and transmission, and many transgender participants at the consultation bravely shared their stories. Intense social stigma and discrimination often affect access to housing, jobs, and education, and can lead to violence and trauma. Many reported limited health care access and a lack of culturally competent health care services, and, in some cases, pursuit of high-risk behaviors, including sex work, to meet basic survival needs.

To address the disparities that exist, the Administration has taken tremendous steps in reducing the inequities transgender people face. This has included the signing of an executive order to prohibit Federal contractors and subcontractors from discriminating on the basis of sexual orientation or gender identity, and the hosting of an LGBTQ Tech & Innovation Summit, which created #TransNeeds, a national online "listening campaign" to identify the needs of transgender Americans.

Ongoing anti-discrimination, research, data collection, training and outreach efforts are also taking place across the Federal government. HHS overall has made strides in including gender identity and sexual orientation on several national surveys. The Department of Defense has started looking at the policy and readiness implications of welcoming transgender people to serve openly in the military. Other agencies have held trainings on gender identity awareness and hate crime prevention.

From the ONAP consultation, it was clear to us that more work must be done to improve HIV outcomes among transgender people, but that the issue is much more complex than one disease and one population. It's layered with issues of stigma, discrimination, the struggle to meet basic needs, and imperfect data, to name a few. We need a wider network of culturally competent providers, increased capacity building and technical support for transgender-focused organizations at the local level, and improved data collection. During the consultation, we kept thinking about a recurring theme around the White House: we are our brothers and sisters' keepers. Thus, we look forward to further efforts address HIV and how we can all work together to improve outcomes among our transgender brothers and sisters.

To learn more, see the CDC fact sheet (included above) *HIV Among Transgender People.*

Amy Lansky, PhD, MPH is Acting Director of the Office of National AIDS Policy.

Raffi Freedman-Gurspan is Outreach & Recruitment Director for Presidential Personnel and Associate Director for Public Engagement at The White House.

Marking Transgender Day of Remembrance

November 20, 2013 at 12:26 PM ET by Gautam Raghavan

Summary:

Today, November 20th, communities across the country and around the world will mark Transgender Day of Remembrance. This day is an opportunity to remember those who have lost their lives to violence and injustice because of their gender identity or gender expression.

Today, November 20th, communities across the country and around the world will mark Transgender Day of Remembrance. This day is an opportunity to remember those who have lost their lives to violence and injustice because of their gender identity or gender expression.

The Obama Administration remains committed to preventing violence against all people, including all members of the LGBT community. Four years ago, President Obama signed the Matthew Shepard and James Byrd Jr. Hate Crime Prevention Act, which greatly expanded the federal government's ability to prosecute hate crimes. The law marked the first time that the words, "sexual orientation" and "gender identity" appeared in the U.S. Code, and enables the Justice Department to prosecute in certain circumstances hate crimes committed because of a person's actual or perceived race, color, religion, national origin, gender, sexual orientation, gender identity, or disability .

In addition, the Department of Justice has worked with transgender advocacy leaders and law enforcement leaders from around the country to create a cultural competency training module that will be delivered by the Department's Community Relations Service (CRS). The training will provide important information to persons interacting with and protecting transgender persons, and will attempt to dispel myths and increase understanding so that communities can better work together to prevent and respond to hate crimes. Interested community groups and law enforcement agencies can reach out to the DOJ's CRS at 202-305-2935 in order to learn more about receiving the training session.

Earlier this year the President was proud to sign a reauthorization of the Violence Against Women Act (VAWA) that included critical protections for transgender people and for the broader LGBT community. The legislation removed barriers faced by LGBT victims of domestic violence and sexual assault, whose needs are often overlooked by law enforcement, prosecutors, courts, and victim service providers. It also included three provisions that would help LGBT victims of domestic violence and sexual assault access VAWA-funded services:

1. First, the law added a LGBT-focused purpose area to the STOP Violence Against Women Formula Grant program, the largest VAWA program and the one that supports law enforcement, prosecution, court and victim service activities in every State.

2. Second, the law amended the Act's definition of "underserved population" to recognize that LGBT victims face barriers to service.

3. Third, the law protects LGBT victims from discrimination by prohibiting discrimination on the basis of sexual orientation or gender identity in VAWA-funded programs or activities.

This commitment to equality for all members of the LGBT community extends internationally, where the Obama Administration continues to promote and protect the human rights of LGBT persons. For example, earlier this year, then-U.S. Ambassador to the United Nations Susan Rice released a video message to mark International Day Against Homophobia, in which she said:

At the United Nations, the United States is standing up for the rights of lesbian, gay, bisexual and transgender individuals and fighting to ensure that their voices are heard and protected. The United States was proud to co-sponsor and adopt an historic resolution at the UN Human Rights Council condemning human rights abuses and violations based on sexual orientation and gender identity.

Today is an opportunity to reflect upon and share the tremendous progress we have made over the last few years. However, let us also recommit ourselves to continuing this critically important work so that we can ensure dignity, equality, and justice for all people.

As President Obama said earlier this year in his LGBT Pride Month remarks at the White House:

> *The genius of America is that America can change. And people who love this country can change it. That's what we're called to do. And I hope that when we gather here next year, and the year after that, we'll be able to say, with pride and confidence, that together we've made our fellow citizens a little more free. We've made this country a little more equal. We've made our world a little more full of love.*

Gautam Raghavan is an Advisor in the White House Office of Public Engagement.

The Michelle Obama Transgender Guide - 46

Index

Transgender Female Health Warnings..........................3
    Facts from the Veterans Administration..............3
    1. COME OUT TO YOUR HEALTH CARE PROVIDER.............3
    2. HORMONE TREATMENT...3
    3. MENTAL HEALTH..4
    4. SUBSTANCE USE/ALCOHOL....................................4
    5. TOBACCO USE...5
    6. SEXUALLY TRANSMITTED INFECTIONS (STIS)...............5
        » HIV/AIDS..5
        » HEPATITIS IMMUNIZATION AND SCREENING.........6
        » HUMAN PAPILLOMA VIRUS (HPV).....................6
    7. CANCER..6
    8. FITNESS (DIET AND EXERCISE)..............................7
    9. HEART HEALTH...7
    10. INTIMATE PARTNER VIOLENCE (IPV)......................7
    11. OLDER TRANSGENDER WOMEN.............................8
    12. KIDNEY DISEASE..8
    YOUR PRIVACY MATTERS...8
    ADDITIONAL RESOURCES...9

HIV Among Transgender People..........................11
    Fast Facts...11
    Terminology..11
    The Numbers...11

The Michelle Obama Transgender Guide - 47

National Center for HIV/AIDS, Viral Hepatitis, STD, and TB Prevention Division of HIV/AIDS Prevention..................13

What CDC Is Doing..14
   Additional Resources..16

I Think I Might Be - Now What Do I Do?.....................17

What Does It Mean to Be Transgender?..........................17
How Do I Know if I'm Transgender?...............................17
Am I Normal?...18
What's It Like to Be Young and Transgender?...................19
Whom Should I Tell?..19
What Will Happen When I Come Out?............................20
What Does It Mean to Transition? Should I Do It?..............21
What Does Being Transgender Mean about My Sexual Orientation? Am I Gay or Straight or What?..................22
What about Sexually Transmitted Infections, HIV, and Pregnancy?...23
How Do I Learn to Like Myself?.....................................25
What Resources Exist for Transgender Youth?...................26

Transgender Military Service Member Policy..............27

Implementation Highlights..27
Policy Highlights..29

OSHA Guide to Restroom Access for Transgender Workers 30

Introduction..30
Understanding Gender Identity....................................30
Why Restroom Access Is a Health and Safety Matter..........31
   OSHA's Sanitation Standard...................................31

   Model Practices for Restroom Access for Transgender Employees...32

Other Federal, State and Local Laws.............................33
   Additional Information..35

   How OSHA Can Help...35

Recognizing the Unique Challenges of Transgender
    Women of Color..37

Our Commitment to Improving Outcomes in the
    Transgender Community..................................40

Marking Transgender Day of Remembrance...............43

Index...46

www.ingramcontent.com/pod-product-compliance
Lightning Source LLC
LaVergne TN
LVHW090443011125
824821LV00035B/338